LIKE MY TEACHER ALWAYS SAID . . .

ERIN McHUGH

LIKE MY TEACHER ALWAYS SAID . . .

Weighty Words, Crazy Wisdom,
the Road to Detention, and Advice We
Could Never Forget, Even If We Tried

ERIN McHUGH

ABRAMS IMAGE
NEW YORK

Editor: David Cashion
Designer: Devin Grosz
Production Manager: Katie Gaffney

Library of Congress Control Number: 2015949273

ISBN: 978-1-4197-2025-3

Printed and bound in the United States
10 9 8 7 6 5 4 3 2 1

Abrams Image books are available at special discounts
when purchased in quantity for premiums and promotions
as well as fundraising or educational use. Special editions
can also be created to specification. For details, contact
specialsales@abramsbooks.com or the address below.

ABRAMS IM▲GE
An imprint of ABRAMS

115 West 18th Street
New York, NY 10011
www.abramsbooks.com

I've had great luck and wonderful experiences with my teachers, from Sister Mary Daniela straight through to Bart Giamatti, but it was the faculty and administration at Skidmore College during the 1970s who taught me the most important lesson: Girls can do anything.

"I love work. I would work for free."

– SUE

CONTENTS

INTRODUCTION

I started out thinking about teachers in a very straight-forward way: as the men and women who stand at the front of our classrooms during our formative years, the folks who keep us in line, somehow teach us fractions, often instill good manners and lifelong values, and scrape the spitballs off the walls at the end of very long days. Along with our parents, they are probably the most important influences leading us down the path—sometimes smooth, often rocky—to our adult selves.

But when I began talking to people about the memories they had of their student years, what I found right away was that the word "teacher" encompasses a much wider group of people than I had originally considered, and that classrooms aren't just in the schoolhouse. Of course, for most of us, the majority of our traditional and formal education happens between the years we toddle off to kindergarten and our near-adult time spent in college—the latter years often spent far from home and under the thrall of the new, exciting ideas presented by our professors rather than the well-worn, oft-repeated ideas our mothers and fathers had been desperately trying to imbue in us. But along the way, we meet other people who are teachers of one sort or another, too.

"Oh, but I want to tell you what my football coach said to me," someone told me. "His advice has stayed with me my whole life." Another said, "My first mentor when I entered the workforce taught me a lesson I've never forgotten—though at the time I was mortified." There were faculty advisors, too, and guidance counselors. And, of course, for students of a certain age and religious background, there were The Nuns. Their reputation precedes them, but the care these women—who had no children of their own—often bestowed on their charges demonstrated that everything wasn't, well, just black and white.

So, my initial notion of what a teacher is grew. And my understanding of what kinds of things they taught us became much vaster. Often, when queried, contributors in this book would initially remember a silly or amusing incident or anecdote from their early school years, then they would stop, consider, and relate a story that has stuck with them well into adulthood. The lessons our teachers impart are countless, the care they give, boundless; the dreams they help us realize, infinite; the hours of listening, endless.

And then there is the very obvious thing that I hadn't considered: Sure the students wanted to tell stories about their teachers and share advice they'd gotten from them—from funny to shocking to wise—but it also turned out that the teachers had plenty to say themselves. They wanted to share what they say to their classes and what they think works in a classroom. A lot of teaching is trial and error, but they didn't at all mind telling tales on themselves. In the end, *Like My Teacher Always Said* . . . turned out to be a warm, hilarious, sweet—and sometimes unnerving!—collection of life in front of the blackboard, with everyone chiming in. It's said that children are our future, but I'll tell you this: Not without our teachers.

Erin McHugh   NEW YORK CITY, SEPTEMBER 2015

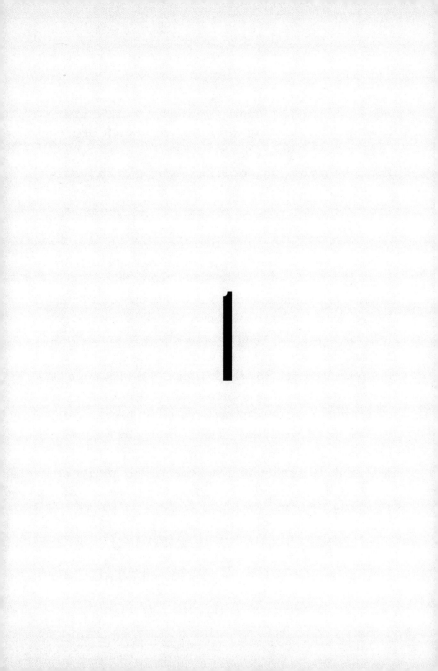

SCARE TACTICS

Any teacher with experience—like, a week's worth of experience—knows that sometimes one of the best ways to keep law and order in the classroom is through instilling a little harmless fear. Nothing crazy or long-lasting to the psyche—just a few tricks to temporarily scare the students straight . . . at least until the bell rings.

My seventh-grade English teacher just loved signs,
I guess. Above the door beneath the clock was:
"Time passes . . . will YOU?" He also had a round
sign hanging from one of the light fixtures that
read "TOIT." His point was that everyone always
says they're going to get AROUND TO IT (a round
TOIT, get it?), but they never do.

– CAIT on Mr. M.

"This paper looks like you dipped a chick in ink
and let it run around your paper," Mrs. K. wrote
on my assignment in the fifth grade. This was right
before she gave me a failing grade in penmanship.
This followed Miss O., my fourth-grade teacher,
who announced to the class that William would
receive the monthly handwriting sample because
he has the worst penmanship she had ever seen. I
will not reveal my age here (though here's a hint:
I'm retired), but it never got any better.

– WILLIAM

I tell every parent with a student from ninth grade and onward: "Don't go away for even a weekend for the next four years."

– SUSAN

The most memorable thing one of my teachers said to me was in kindergarten. She said, "Mind your own business." I had simply asked why there was a sixth grader sitting on a stool in a corner facing the wall in our classroom. I was stricken! I grew up to be an author, and I have always wondered if that incident had something to do with the fact that I have spent almost my entire career asking (and answering) questions.

– ERIC on Mrs. B.

My high school chemistry
teacher used to tell us, "Carol
never wore her safety goggles.
Now, she doesn't need them."
It was a joke. I think. But it sure
got the point across.

– ALICIA on Mr. P.

My second-grade teacher, Mr. K., had me pegged
from the start. He was constantly after me, saying,
"You had better settle down and settle down FAST!"

– LEIGH on Mr. K.

I teach pre-K, and I get some kids with real potty
mouths, even at that age. I'm never going to be
able to eradicate it, but I try to make a dent.

"You're not allowed to say bad words unless you're
eighteen," I tell them. "How old are you?"
"Four," they'll say. "Five."
"OK, no bad words, then. You can say them when
you are eighteen."
"Do you say bad words?" they want to know next.
"Not when I'm with you guys," I say, reminding
them, "because you're four."

– DIANA

In my years of teaching, I would tell anyone who
put his or her head down on a desk that I would
remove the desk if it happened again, and, "When
your head hits the floor, it will be quite a mess."

– BILL

I will never forget how our tiny elementary school teacher Mrs. G. terrified us, especially when she stood on a chair in front of the class waving a ruler frantically and shouting, "I am going to annihilate you!" as her face turned beet red. Bewildered and terrified little creatures that we were, we had no idea what the meaning of "annihilate" was or what fate was destined to befall us. But we got the picture—it wasn't good! And we were good kids!

Contrast that with my kindergarten teacher, the beautiful Mrs. R., with a huge blonde pompadour, who played the piano and sang childhood favorites as we rolled out our little blankets on the floor at naptime. Inspiring? Maybe not to anyone else, but the wonderful energy of Mrs. R. and the memorable images of that sunlit room at naptime bring tears to my eyes decades later.

– LILLIAN

"Just think what you could do
if you only applied yourself."

- TOO MANY TEACHERS TO COUNT to Michael
....

2

ADVICE THAT STUCK

Frequently with life lessons or special moments, you don't even realize they're happening until some time—often years—has gone by. Such is often the case for students: Anything from an important ethical point to the most off-handed comment can stick with a pupil and become a watchword or standard for a lifetime.

I had a math teacher who said to me: "The finish line will always be there. Just finish the run." I had a habit of starting to solve equations but never finishing them, even though I was on the right track.

– ASHLEY on Mrs. D.

Over the years, I have frequently thought about the words of a professor of mine, and have often quoted him to my colleagues at work. Here's what happened . . .

A classmate of mine raised her hand in class and said, "Dr. C., I don't have all the information I need to make this decision."

Dr. C. replied, "If you had all the information you needed, there wouldn't be a decision to make. Decisions are about making a choice of what to do based on what you know, and what you think is the best course."

– BRIAN on Dr. C.

"Hard work beats talent
every time, and brings
talent to new levels."

– MR. G. to Dylan

"Dare to be different," Mrs. H.
said to me in high school when
I began hanging with some
"not-so-good" kids.

– MARILYN on Mrs. H.

"Never pass the first clean bathroom stall," my kindergarten teacher taught us. As you can imagine, it has become a valuable piece of advice throughout life.

– ALICIA on Mrs. T.

Dateline: Clearwater, Florida. The high school basketball coach also doubled as the driver's education teacher—not an unusual double duty for public schools. I rear-ended a fellow student while driving in a circle in the parking lot during second-period driver's ed because I was too busy talking to my friend Debbie, who was in the passenger seat. Of course I was in trouble, but what I remember most about that day is coach's saying, "You do realize that the whole school is going to know about this by the end of the day, and that it's going to turn into a six-car pileup?" It was the wisdom of how gossip works in a high school. And he was right.

– MICHELLE on Coach W.

I had a tenth-grade English teacher who taught early American literature—*The Last of the Mohicans*, *The Scarlet Letter*, and all that. She made a big deal out of handing out the next tattered paperback we would be reading and encouraging everyone to really focus in on the "trappings" of the book. I don't think this is the proper term, but in her context, it was all of a book's "stuff" before page one and after the final page. She taught us to pay close attention to all of that stuff, and closely read dedications, opening quotations, author's notes . . . every bit of it. At the time, it just seemed like more work, but this is something I definitely still do today. And many times I make interesting connections or learn something helpful for reading before the story even starts.

— ELIZABETH on Mrs. B.

Ms. T. always said, "Read, always read. Let a book be a friend who is always true, a love who is always faithful, and a dream that you'll always remember."

— WILLIAM on Ms. T.

"You are not going to
learn it by osmosis."

– MR. N. to Steve

"Good, better, best, never let it
rest, till the good is better and
the better is the best!"

– MRS. S. to Dianne

"Inch by inch, life's a cinch."

– MRS. H. to her students

I had a drawing professor my freshman year of college who was known for yelling (maybe screaming) harsh realities at students during model-drawing sessions. The only thing he ever yelled at me was, "You can't get by on talent alone!" which was terrifying and confusing to my eighteen-year-old self. I think my professor was mostly just messing with me, but was probably also referring to hard work and determination. Being able to draw well isn't enough to make creative success.

– MARTHA on Mr. D.

When my mother called a meeting with my teacher about my handwriting, my teacher said, "Don't worry about *how* she writes, worry about *what* she writes." Now my own daughter's handwriting is—how shall I put this?—*terrible*, and it's amazing how often I remind myself of this episode.

– TINA on Ms. L.

In the fifth grade, after winning the spelling bee (even spelling better than sixth graders!), *Miz* E. (in the south we said "Ms." before it was official) said to me, "Just because you can spell, doesn't mean you are smart." This maybe isn't the best teacher comment I ever got, but it did kind of motivate me. Miz E. also taught us some tried-and-true memory tricks. They may have sounded sort of dumb at the time, but I use them still, subconsciously or not:

"Fri your friend and that's the end."

(How to spell "friend" correctly)

"Connect—I—cut"

(How to spell Connecticut)

"In fourteen hundred and ninety-two, Columbus sailed the ocean blue."

(Not original to her, but it still worked!)

But most of all, I remember that she gave a math test every day.

– SESSALEE on Miz E.

As an adult, I have been a student of printmaking for the last few years, and the best advice I've ever gotten was from a teacher who was encouraging me to take more risks and to not try to make everything a masterpiece. He'd remind me, "It's just a piece of paper."

– SANDY on Mr. D.

My eighth-grade language arts teacher came back from lunch in a bit of a huff. She wrote on the board: "Je'et?" and then, "No, ju?"

She explained that this was the "conversation" that she had just overheard two students having in the hallway. She was peeved that our language was being trimmed down to syllables instead of including the whole words. The students meant to say, "Did you eat?" and, "No, did you?" This has stuck with me for all these years, and I still find myself paying attention to every syllable when I speak.

– CHRISTINE on Ms. L.

I had an architecture professor who always warned us, "Water and wood, no good," meaning the use of wood in a home or building near the ocean, or in areas with lots of rain and snow, was not a wise idea. If the architects, builders, homeowners, and others I've worked with as a designer and developer over the years had adhered to those five words, they would have saved quintillions of dollars, as well as time and untold aggravation.

– PETER on Mr. Z.

Every. Single. Day. Our high school principal did the morning announcements and Every. Single. Day. He ended with, "Today is the first day of the rest of your life. Make it a good one." Of course, as teenagers, we rolled our eyes, but I haven't forgotten it. I may not always live it, but I haven't forgotten it.

– BARBARA on Mr. L.

"Character is what you do
when no one is looking."

– MR. B. to Aidan

3

CRAZYTOWN

Sure, we'd love to think that every class went according to plan, that every teacher forever kept his cool, that there was never a moment (or many) where things got out of control—waaay out of control—but that's not life, is it?

So, Mr. C. shows up in class with a black eye.

Me: "Hey, Mr. C. . . . what happened to your eye?"

Mr. C.: "I fell down some stairs."

Me: "No, seriously, how'd you get that black eye?"

Mr. C.: "You want one?"

Me: "No."

Mr. C.: "Then I fell down some stairs."

– JOEY on Mr. C.

My wood shop teacher in middle school was missing half of a finger on one hand. If you were not paying attention in class, he would hold up his hand and say, "This is what you get for inky-dinkying around!"

– MICHAEL on Mr. F.

During dances at my
Episcopalian boarding school,
Miss D. would break up close
dancing with, "Make room for
the Holy Ghost."

– HILDA on Miss D.

"Sing out, Louise!" is a famous line from the musical *Gypsy*. My high school drama teacher would say it to any student, at any moment, in any class, in any rehearsal, in any non-theatrical situation. Now . . . she's probably saying it to a cashier or waiter right this moment.

– DOUG on Mrs. W.

I had a brilliant and animated French teacher for all four years of high school. She regularly quoted Frost and Dante's *Inferno* (yes), though her original quips were just as great. She was not a nun, but we were at a Catholic school, and in every class, before praying, she would announce, "When you pray in French, the prayers go *straight to heaven!*"

– MARTHA on Madame C.

If he really liked something, my junior high band teacher would say, "That worked slicker than snot on a doorknob!"

– JOAN on Mr. S.

After gym class, our teacher would always say, with a full-blown Long Island accent, "Allright, ya buncha B.O.s, hit the showahs!"

– DIANE on Mrs. D.

My fifth-grade homeroom teacher was Mrs. E. She was an older lady—probably 50! *yuk, yuk*—and had a shrewish/prunish face so ugly and severe that you could see she was mean even before she showed it to be true. We knew it from the first day of school—though she was legend before we even got to her classroom, of course. Mrs. E. kept her own upright piano in the classroom and loved to stage endless sessions where she would play and we would sing—her signature tune was "The Wabash Cannonball."

One day, Mrs. E. was bawling out one poor kid about something or other, I don't remember what, and another kid named Sammy was standing right behind her, doing a great pantomime of her shrieking and finger-wagging. Suddenly, one of the girls—it was always a girl—who was observing Sammy's acting prowess over Mrs. E.'s shoulder said, "Oh Mrs. E.," (lilting up-note) "Sammy is mimicking you." Snitch!

Mrs. E. spun around on one heel like a pivoting fury and thrust her nasty beak right into Sammy's face. Then, eyes *blazing*, she started stabbing her two clawlike hands into his face, repeatedly, ending in a sharp clap just as you thought she was going to put out his eyes, and screaming: "*YOU*"–JAB . . . CLAP!–"mimic MEEEEEEE??!!"– STAB . . . CLAP!–"How dare you??!!"–JAB . . . CLAP!–"WHY . . . YOU'RE NOT FIT TO WIPE MY BOOTS!!!!"–STAB . . . CLAP!

An interesting choice of words on her part. The expression gave something away about her age, because I guess by "boots," she meant high-buttoned shoes, of which she probably had a collection in her closet. To us kids, she was the Wicked Witch of the West come to life at our little elementary school.

I've never forgotten the incident, and it made a great and lasting impression on me. This lady was truly out of control, fire in her eyes, and there was no telling what might happen next, which made it particularly scary—and, of course, exhilarating.

– LEO on Mrs. E.

It wasn't what Miss P. said so much as what she did. If a student did something bad, she would hang him or her, by belt loop or collar, on one of the coat hooks that were around the room for our little jackets. How long? Well, it seemed like an eternity, but the punishment lasted about a half hour. Which was an eternity.

– VERONICA on Miss P.

After a delightful pre-school
meal of Manischewitz with
a friend in ninth grade,
my teacher Mrs. G. asked
what I had for breakfast.
"Cereal," I replied.
"Tomorrow you might want to
add some toast," she replied.
Today, of course, I would be
sent to a home for wayward
children immediately.

– MARTHA on Mrs. G.

4

WISE WORDS

Every teacher's career has boasted both some worthy wisdom and some choice zingers. But one question always remains: Do the students remember how smart and clever you were? Here, some teachers share their prize insights, and some former students share their favorite memories.

I went back to college after forty years, and my dean—and now dear friend—gave me some sound academic advice regarding course selection during my first semester: "Michael, at your age, it's OK to eat dessert first."

– MICHAEL on Professor L.

"It's nice to be important—but more important to be nice!"

– MRS. P. to Helen

Whenever my class started acting up, I always tried to get them in line by saying, "C'mon, kids! We've got oceans to cross and mountains to climb."

– MRS. H.

Over the years, when I have spoken with parents—
either at school open houses or in individual
meetings—I have tried to talk to them about
the benefits of social responsibility and service
learning. In my experience, when I ask parents
what they want for their child's future, many will
say they want their child to be happy. Others will
say they want their child to be successful. What
I have come to believe is that we should strive to
want our children to be not happy or successful,
but good—that if they are good people, they will
find happiness and success.

– SUE

When my students ask me how long their essays
should be, I always tell them that they should be
like a skirt: long enough to cover the subject, but
short enough to keep it interesting.

– DIANNE

My Latin teacher used to say, "Common sense is not very common." I still cite this quite often, many, many years later.

– STEVE on Mr. D.

I'll always remember my sixth-grade teacher's pep talk about moving into the city's junior high school from our little neighborhood grammar school. "Always remember, the kings here are the queens there. Be brave!"

– HOWARD on Mr. P.

As a college consultant, I tell students, "Don't let those kids who say or act like they already have everything all figured out scare you. They actually have nothing figured out. They just don't know it yet, so in that way, you're ahead of the game."

– ELIZABETH

"You can wear a burlap sack, but you will be judged on your vocabulary."

– MISS M. to Denise

I had a high school math teacher who was devilishly handsome, but always seemed hungover and deeply unhappy . . . in a really sexy, James Dean kind of way. All the girls were wild about him. He'd give us some equations or whatever to do in class, and every time, he would say, in this suicidal, existential tone of voice, "Chop-chop-lotta-work. Work-makes-life-sweet." It was funny because it was so weird, but I did end up remembering it, didn't I? And so did everyone I went to high school with. And now I think he's right.

– ERIN on Mr. G.

My college French teacher answered questions with, "It's clear as mud, but it covers the ground."

– SIMONE on Monsieur C.

My second-grade teacher always said, "Mind your B . . . hold your T . . . do your W . . . and you'll be done!"

– BETSY on Mrs. M.

At the end of each day, Mrs. G. would ask the class, "Did you learn something today?" Of course, the class would inevitably respond with a resounding "Yes!" to which Mrs. G. would inevitably reply, "Well then, please take it with you!"

– ZACH on Mrs. G.

My mom had an "Art Rap" she would teach her students. Now she has those same students' kids come up to her and sing the song. . . .

"You can't, You can't mess up in art!

You can fix it if you're smart,

Or you can turn it over for a fresh start BUT

You can't, You can't mess up in art!

So don't throw it away save a tree today BECAUSE

You can't, You can't mess up in art!

You need help you say? Well PLEASE and THANK YOU is the only way

Because, You can't, You can't mess up in art!

So remember kids, what did Ms. S. say?

You can't, You can't mess up in art!"

– JILL on her mother Janis, the art teacher

My kids' kindergarten teacher always said "Hocus pocus, TIME TO FOCUS!"—and I still use that with my scatterbrained youngest to this day.

– MELISSA on Ms. K.

My junior high typing teacher:

"When in danger, when in doubt,
Run in circles, scream and shout,
Hit the ceiling, hit the floor,
Then throw yourself right out the door!"

The message was, when you have a problem, instead of freaking out, find a way to deal with it yourself.

– STEFFANIE on Mr. E.

Through my years as a teacher, I've found I say these three things over and over again:

"Start with what you do know, and then build from there."

"The most challenging questions start with 'How' or 'Why.'"

"This is a classroom, not your living room."

– JULIET

My AP English teacher told me that he didn't mind my sleeping in class; however, he requested that I fall asleep before he *started*.

– JEFF on Mr. B.

Memories from my early teacher days—I have long been an administrator, but I think they still hold true!

I encouraged my students to be kind—especially to me. I told them it was good for them to give me compliments, like "You look nice today," "What nice shoes you have," and "What a good haircut." I know it sounds like Eddie Haskell, but it was OK with me, even if they didn't mean it. It made me happier.

I told my students they were the BEST! They always were the best. I loved teaching them and they knew it.

I wanted my students to be successful, both inside and outside of my classroom. I encouraged them to take risks and to travel and to debate and to be physically active. I tried to demonstrate all those things, too.

I talked about my family and let my students know what was going on in my life, and I learned as much as I could about their lives. Often, they would reveal personal things in their essays and I was careful to honor what they told me.

I hooted out loud when I made a mistake or did something silly. There was always laughter and silliness in my classroom.

I taught a lot of vocabulary in those days—and instead of the usual way, I had all the students stand up (no leaning on the desk, they had to stand upright!) and I'd ask them, one by one, for the proper definition. If they got it right, they could sit down and we moved on. They loved to sit, so they studied! We went around and around. "Still standing" meant that the student hadn't studied. The class loved it. It worked. It was a safe environment, so this wasn't a painful thing.

I changed the configuration of the classroom almost every day. The students didn't know what to expect—groups of four, two half circles, rows alphabetically. . . . Every day all of the students had to find their name cards on their newly assigned spots.

– SUSAN

Here are some things my teachers said to me over the years:

"Try your best."

"Try harder."

"Take your time."

"You have to think."

"Add it up."

"Take some away."

And here are some of the things I say, as a teacher, to my students:

"Do not use the word 'bored,' because you can't be BORED if you have something to do, and someone to do it with."

"Take your time."

"Do not worry about right or wrong, just do your best."

"Be kind and be safe."

"You can't say you can't play."

"When you have hurt someone, after you say you're sorry, ask him if he is OK."

"Do your own work."

"Did you check for capitals and punctuation?"

– MEG

My principal always said,
"School is not a dress
rehearsal for life."

– ELLIE on Mrs. G.

5

IT'S FUNNY
BECAUSE IT'S TRUE

We all have those times from school: nutty moments we've never forgotten, stories we tell decades later. Whether it's something we did, something the teacher said, or a time when things just fell apart, each of these moments had the same effect: laughter. The question usually is: Who was left speechless more often—the teacher or the students?

In my high school Spanish class, my teacher, Señora L., a native of Uruguay, said to me—all Chita Rivera-like—"ROBERTO! You are not concentrated!"

When I was in graduate school for photography, I spent a summer studying at Agfa, a film company in Munich. The German lecturer who was delivering a very technical dissertation could not believe the blank expressions on all of our faces. With total exasperation, he said, "You must, you must, tell me what you don't know."

I was always getting caught for sort of "double-dipping" on my free time. More than once I heard (correctly), "Didn't you have lunch last period?"

—AIISHA on Mr. Z.

My freshman year, we had this male biology teacher. Big dude, a booming voice, and it seemed like he always talked at half speed. Inevitably, we arrived at the always-embarrassing human reproduction chapter. He stood up in front of class and said, "I . . . am . . . a walking . . . uterus. THEEEEEESE"—pointing to his arms—"are my fallopian tuuuuuubes." It went on from there, and as I'm now in my forties, you can see it made a lasting impression.

— MELISSA on Mr. C.

Mrs. G., our truly amazing and inspiring history teacher, who used to go on about her childhood as a refugee in war-torn England, always lectured in a combination lisp and rather demonstrative Oxford-educated accent.

One day, during a lecture on some decisive point in European History, she was talking about the common man pulling himself up "by his jockstraps" (when she obviously meant *bootstraps*). The look on her face when she realized her mistake was priceless. We all broke into laughter and chortles seconds ahead of her realizing what she'd said. Her face turned a full-on English Rose, but she appreciated the joke.

– ROBERT on Mrs. G.

My high school English teacher, Mr. S., told me I had "a complicated relationship" with commas. It remains so all these years later. And I remain friends with Mr. S. Thankfully, he hasn't held the comma complications against me—and it didn't hurt my writing career!

– ERIC on Mr. S.

When my students have figured something out, I always say, "You're so smart. Kiss your brain!"

– RENATA

My sixth-grade English
teacher was amazing. She
wore red Chuck Taylors and
matching funky red glasses.
She called sixth graders
"worms" and seventh
graders "weenies." I can't
remember what she
called eighth graders, but it
was surely a small step up
from the other names.

— KIRSTIN on Ms. B.

I've been an ob-gyn for many years now, but
I'll never forget what one of my surgical teachers
would tell us: "Try not to grab defeat from the
jaws of victory!"

– DR. FREDDY on Dr. H.

**I was only in kindergarten, and
my teacher was already saying,
"Your mouth is like diarrhea;
it just runs and runs."**

– JEAN on Mrs. P.

"You've got to stop talking or I'm going to call your mother," Mrs. R. said to me. And then she actually followed through on her threat and called. My mother's response: "Stop talking!"

– SARA on Mrs. R.

I guess a was a picky eater as a kid, because every single day Miss B. would open my lunchbox and say, "Finish your lunch. I'm going to stand here until you eat it." And then, one day, I threw up, and she never asked me again.

– ELLIE on Miss B.

In my fourth-grade science class, Mrs. M. said, "Everything that moves makes noise." I shot my hand up and said, "Runs in your stockings don't make noise." I can't remember how she handled my comment, but she didn't get angry, and was able to move right along with her lesson plan.

– SUSIE on Mrs. M.

If there's such a thing as accountant humor, Mr. B., my accounting professor in business school, was a master. He was a former chief enforcer at the SEC before becoming a teacher. He liked to say, "Anyone can make a mistake, but it takes a computer to really f**k things up."

Another favorite of his was:

Q: How does an accountant describe a plane crash?
A: Premature retirement of aircraft.

– JACK on Mr. B.

I had a history teacher in grade school who would just get so exasperated with all of us when we weren't paying attention that she would say, "Stop the world, I want to get off." She never actually left the room, but we got the picture. When she needed a respite from us, instead of showing a movie like a normal wrung-out teacher, she played tapes from motivational speaker and author Zig Ziglar—still the only exposure I've had of him to date.

She looked like she was fresh out of the civil rights movement and had been plopped into a small-town Texas classroom. She didn't teach us the history of Texas—which it seemed was the only history we were required to know—so much as she taught Texas trivia. I swear I didn't know who the Redcoats were until I went to college and found out about the American Revolution, but I did know the six flags of Texas (France, Spain, the Confederate States of America, the Republic of Texas, Mexico, and the United States of America); the state flower (bluebonnet); the state bird (mockingbird); and the state tree (pecan). What I didn't know about was anywhere else.

— SHANNON on Mrs. K.

Miss E. told us that there were only two excuses for not finishing her (extremely copious) homework: sickness or a young man.

6

COACHES, MENTORS & OTHER UNFORGETTABLES

When we say the word "teacher," we're not always talking about the person standing in front of the classroom. The lessons we learn can come from a whole army of people: the person in front of the blackboard; the coach on the field, in the gym, on the water; guidance counselors; even therapists and mentors we meet as adults. Because if you're doing life right, you never stop learning.

I grew up around books. My father read, my mother read, there were books and bookshelves everywhere in our house.

My mother worked at an ad agency (hello, *Mad Men*). This was the sixties. That meant that when school ended, I couldn't go home, because there was no one there (this was pre-latchkey kids). So I had to go somewhere.

I could walk to the public library or I could walk from my last class to the school library. Most often, I chose the second option: the school library.

Why? Helen M., the school librarian. She was spectacularly elegant: hair, clothes, jewelry, nails. I was in awe of her. I don't think she realized that she was my babysitter. She gave me a task: shelve returned books. So, that's what I did most days after school: shelve returned books.

Here's what Mrs. M. told me: Every book you shelve has been read and touched by a hundred hands. Honor them.

— SUSAN on Mrs. M.

As both a teacher and
a coach, my motto is,
"Practice makes better."

– SUZANNE

My family is full of athletes. I was a gymnast grow-
ing up, and my dad was a very gung-ho wrestling
coach. When he'd drop me off at practice, he'd
say, "Break the bar!" meaning I should go so hard
that I'd damage the uneven bars. Now, I have a
baby girl of my own, and when I overheard my hus-
band telling her to "Break the bar!" I almost lost it.

– LINDSAY on Coach (and Dad) M.

My gymnastics coach always cautioned, "If you rest, you rust."

– BARB on Mr. A.

My tennis coach used to tell us, "Winning is a frame of mind." She must have been right, because her tennis team won thirty consecutive seasons, and was featured in *Sports Illustrated*.

– SUSAN on Mrs. B.

I think that my favorite thing my mentor, N., has said to me was, "Stand back and take a look." What she meant was to keep my perspective, and not get too high or too low.

– ELISA

During a conversation about why I had left my
job following a fight with cancer, and how I
had decided, after all I'd been through, that a
particular job wasn't for me, and how it was time
to turn to music as my career, I got some of the
best advice of my life. This is what S., a musician
and a great mentor of mine, said to me in a hotel
the morning before our second show at the famed
Bowery Ballroom in New York City.

"How we got here doesn't really matter, we just
need to be the best at what we are today. If I'm a
singer in a band, I'm going to be the best damn
singer I can be. If I'm a hotel employee, I'm going
to be the best hotel employee they've ever had."

– JON on S.

"Swing the pendulum," Coach T. used to say to me.
What he meant was, whatever someone throws at
you, push right back.

– KAREN on Coach T.

I'm an educational counselor, and when my students head off to college, I always tell them: "Enjoy it all. Be safe. Learn something. But if you are truly lucky, you'll look back on your whole life and not actually feel that college was the best four years you had." (So no pressure.)

– ELIZABETH

"Slow down—you'll have more time."

– Tennis instructor MR. V. to Mal

"The next time you take a year off from college, don't register for classes!" ("I didn't go to class much!" admits Shelley.)

– MR. H., faculty advisor, to Shelley

"Do something significant today. You can sleep when you're dead."

– Trainer RICH to Lisa

From my college vocal coach: "Learn all repertoire by heart to sing from the heart. If you're chained to the page, the music and lyrics will be compromised. Do your homework; practice, practice, practice. Sing from memory. The music and lyrics lie in your interpretation and will only live in you and through you when you give them their due."

I still teach—and live—by this sound method.

– DENISE on Sister C.

My high school football coach described fair-weather fans as "the same people who wouldn't pay a nickel to see the Statue of Liberty urinate."

– PAT on Coach B.

I am a college counselor at an all-girls high school and, of course, my students run the gamut from struggling to brilliant. But year after year, I give them all the same advice, and it's the advice my father always gave me: "Hold your head high."

– MRS. B.

When I was just starting out in business, I had a mentor at the corporation I worked for named Mr. L., who told us: "Enemies become friends to make it a larger industry!"

– JOHN on Mr. L.

What better teacher than
your shrink? "You have all
the time there is," mine
would say to me quietly
whenever I used the excuse,
"I don't have time for that!"

– MOLLY on Dr. C.

I am a rowing coach, so I
make sure I tell all my kids,
"I brake for seals."

– BETTS

On my first day at Doubleday, then the world's largest book publisher, I was assigned to write the flap copy for a book entitled (I kid you not—in fact it went on to be a big bestseller) *The Power of Prayer on Plants*.

Not yet far removed from my English-major idea of publishing, I couldn't believe Doubleday would publish such a manuscript. But I wrote the copy, turned it in to my boss, and got on an elevator with a fellow trainee. "You won't believe . . ." I started out, and told him what a crazy day I'd had and what nonsense was being peddled by our employer. The elevator door opened, and as I was getting out, a very dapper man standing behind me tapped on my shoulder and said, "Don't talk in elevators."

It was, of course, the executive editor of Doubleday, the book's editor, and a man I was sure would get me fired the next day.

Fortunately, he liked the flap copy and cut me some slack. In fact, he became something of a mentor to me. But I tell you, I never talked in an elevator again.

In his time, my mentor edited more bestselling fiction than anyone else.

– LEE on his mentor, also named Lee

"Practice doesn't make perfect. Perfect practice makes perfect."

– Coach **TIM** to Allison

7

THE SISTERS

Oh, the dying breed that suffered so long at the hands of their tormentors! Kids today have never experienced the habits, the rulers, the terror that was life in a Catholic school during the twentieth century. This subset of teachers had free rein in raising children, with no backtalk brooked from either students or their parents. Were they doing the best they could while potentially being stifled in an unusual way of life? Very likely. But nevertheless, the stories live on. . . .

For years, the Sisters of Mercy told me I was "a bold little stump!!" (I understood the negativity, but what exactly *is* a bold little stump, I've always wondered.) Then, in seventh grade, I had Sister M. C. T. for a teacher. I don't recall much of what she *said* to me, but what this nun *did* for me was extraordinary: She gave me extra-curricular reading—stuff that a seventh-grade girl in the sixties would be interested in. We'd meet every two weeks or so to discuss books that were well off the beaten, required track. Gothic novels, romance, etc. I felt singled out, special, and she was the initial inspiration of my lifelong love of reading. Years later, I figured that she probably was trying to take that "bold little stump" and divert her revolutionary energy into more acceptable diversions! She certainly succeeded in both areas!

– ANNE on Sister M. C. T.

"DON'T LOOK AT ME IN THAT TONE OF VOICE."

– SISTER W. to Rob

"A definite no today may save you trouble and heartache tomorrow." This was the message sent in a newsletter to all parents in my high school advising them to not allow their girls to go away to the beach on a class vacation immediately following graduation. At that point, even the chaperones were all lined up to come along. We all assumed this was some enforced type of Catholic birth control.

– MICHELE on a note from Mother Superior

After a certain point in my freshman year, my principal, Sister A., called me in and said, "Let's save some paper, Mary Seton. ASSUME you have detention unless you hear otherwise." I even spent Saturdays folding napkins in the basement of the convent.

Recently, Sister A. came to see me in a dream when I was ill, appearing like a beacon—or maybe a nightmare. What was she doing here? There couldn't possibly be more detention. I had served my time. "It's not all fun is it, Mary Seton?" she said. "Not everything is a joke, people are depending on you to make decisions. They need you." I assumed she was speaking about my business and the folks who worked for me. But why was she back to bother me? I had been, after all, her Achilles' heel. Everyone knew that. I was always out of uniform. I stole the teachers' bathroom key over and over and placed it right inside my locker with a sign that said "Teachers' Bathroom Key Here." She knew. I knew she knew. She never stooped down to my level though. Sister

A. didn't stoop to anyone's level. Teachers, parents, the Holy Father, the students, we were all afraid of her. She never raised her voice. She never threw things. She was just herself.

One week, word came down that Sister A.'s father had died. We had never thought of her as a person with a family; we thought she had arrived on earth fully formed as Sister A. I didn't like the idea of funerals and I knew this would be a mandatory all-school mass. I just did not want to go and I felt strongly about it. I girded myself and said to her, "Sister, I'm sorry about your loss, but I don't like funerals and I don't believe in God. I cannot attend your father's funeral mass." I waited for the wrath. As usual she had no expression. And then she touched my shoulder, looked me in the eye, and said, "You are excused from mass today, Mary Seton. I'm sure you'll find something useful to do in the library. You will be unsupervised." I realized I had a chance to show her what I was really made of. She knew in that moment that there was more to me, and in that moment I knew it, too. When I graduated from high school, at the very bottom of my class, I received the principal's award—the highest honor in the school. We shook hands solemnly as my classmates and the teachers cheered. "Mary won!" they screamed. I had brought down the wicked witch! But had I really? In that one moment, she had changed my life. She had made me understand that to lead, you had to love. You had to be bigger than anything around you. You had to find the way in the dark. You had to care. Leading was not edicts, it was caring about the people you led, always introducing the intangibles of life into the equation, always wanting to do the right thing.

I didn't go out to change the world that graduation day. It would take many decades before I introduced the word "we" into my vocabulary. But when I did, it came out naturally. I knew who I was and I was ready to do what I knew I could do, what I was meant to do: to lead.

– MARY SETON on Sister A.

My teachers always told me that I would be a success no matter my career choice, and I that would make a difference in others' lives. They believed in me, and so I believed in me.

– PAULETTE on Sister A. C. and Sister Mary P.

I'll never forget Sister J.
chasing one miscreant boy
around the room, shouting,
"You'll pay the fiddler, Ralph!"

– ELLEN on Sister J.

"You are a smart girl, but you'll never hold a candle to your mother." Yes, unfortunately, my sixth-grade teacher also taught my mom.

– ANN on Sister Mary C.

"You brazen hussy, you!" Sister Mary K. used to tell me when I was a kid. Let me tell you, at that point, I was too young to even understand what a hussy was, never mind act like one!

– MIMI on Sister Mary K.

Sister C.: "What are you girls doing?"

Us: "Nothing."

Sister C.: "You're giggling."

Us: [more giggling]

Sister C.: "You must be smoking those funky cigarettes."

We were not, in fact, and that made us laugh even harder, which I'm sure convinced Sister C. of our malfeasance even more.

– VERONICA on Sister C.

When students were sent to visit our principal, Sister W. A., for serious infractions of the rules, she would ask them "What do YOU think your punishment should be?" and inevitably the punishments they recommended for themselves were always worse than the ones she thought they should receive. This always made her smile.

– DIANE on Sister W. A.

I grew up in Ireland in the sixties, when the nuns did not fool around. For those souls brave and foolish enough to argue, we were told:

1. "We'll give you a receipt for your teeth."
2. "We'll hang you by your tonsils."
3. "We'll dye your eye."

– VIV

In the fifth grade, Sister J. had me sit in her desk drawer for an hour as punishment for talking to my friend Virginia. Her reasoning: "Maybe your numb behind will remind you to numb your tongue."

– STELLA on Sister J.

In an attempt to make us walk up the stairs quietly, my French teacher would always say, "Walk up the stairs with velvet paws." Of course, it sounded so glamorous in French that it worked pretty well.

– DENISE on Sister J. M.

When I was in high school in the seventies, there was a nun who was so crazed about Communists that she thought there was a submarine in the school pond. She was constantly warning us to stay away for our own good. There was a pipe of some kind that stuck out of the middle of the pond, and this was apparently the periscope of a sophisticated Communist observation scheme. How they managed to get the submarine *into* the pond was never known, nor was she clear on why they would want to spy on a Catholic high school, but perhaps that's much more believable if you lived through any of that cold war stuff. Or maybe it was just Sister L.

– JEANNINE on Sister L.

In my experience, the sisters had an odd *habit* (sorry!) of addressing you by your sex, rather than your name. And they had some catch phrases that got used over and over again. With Sister A., it was always:

"Girl, you're fresh as wet paint!"
or
"Boy, you're as bold as all outdoors!"

The kicker, though, was the time Francis Y. pulled one over on Sister X. when he used a whoopee cushion during Mass:

"Boy, if you're sick, you go to the nurse."

– MICHAEL on Sister A.

Believe it or not, I was well into my forties before I finally understood where nuns came from. I thought they were from—where, Texas? Portugal? Mars? I had no idea that they were local girls, often from large families who couldn't afford to educate every child. So it now makes sense to me that their biggest put-down when they thought you were getting too big for your britches was to say:

"You think you are God's gift to New Bedford!"

That was the city we lived in, and to us little kids in the fifties and sixties, it was our whole world—now I realize it was the sisters' world, too. Half a century ago, people didn't fly around for vacations, and rarely did our fathers go on faraway business trips. Funny, now, to think of our teachers browbeating us with that phrase—my childhood friends and I still laugh about it because it seems such an absurd statement. But in second grade, it felt global to both the students and the teachers.

– ERIN

"Go to a non-Catholic college
and you will lose your faith."

– EVERY NUN EVER, according to Ellen

8

DIFFERENT DRUMMERS

_____

The insightful teacher—the one who's really watching—will always see the kid who, for one reason or another, is not the same as the rest of the class. Smarter, odder, shyer, more inventive, they just *know*, and make sure to give that student a push in the right direction. And let's face it, sometimes the insightful educators are the teachers who march to that different beat, and their students are all the better for it.

I adored my sixth-grade English teacher. When I
look back on it now, he must have been all of twenty-
five years old, but a grownup to me, of course. This
was in 1979–80. The song "Rapper's Delight,"
which is now considered the first big hip-hop song,
had just come out. He let us spend much of the first
half of the year learning all of the words to the song,
and then deconstructing it to teach us grammar and
syntax. Another teaching method was using Mad
Libs in class.

– ABBE on Mr. K.

After saying something laced with profanity in an
acting class, I felt I had to apologize. My fabulous
acting teacher (whom I adore to this day for
celebrating me exactly as I was) said to me: "Oh
Emily! Don't apologize. Profanity is your essence!"
He nailed it!

– EMILY on Dev

My seventh-grade health teacher used to say, "Water is the champagne of life."

– JILL on Ms. H.

My very favorite teacher was very respectful and smart. He could be a little racy, but was never icky. He was one of my high school heroes. He was a Korean War vet with a metal plate in his head who would do a headstand on his desk to reward us if we were enthusiastic in class. I went to a huge high school and felt pretty invisible, but he made me feel noticed and smart. I miss him.

– BARB on Mr. D.

This is a situation where a teacher's silence won over every kid in the school.

Mr. B., the headmaster at my kids' school, was a tall, gawky, glasses-wearing professorial type who used words in daily assemblies that very smart kids all had to go look up later. He was also a former Army Ranger, and my kids still talk about the day that there was some sort of karate demonstration during daily assembly and the muscle-bound jerk running it said to Mr. B., "Go ahead and try to knock me over." A mild-mannered guy, the headmaster gave him a polite little shove. "You can do better than that," the guy sneered. Mr. B. continued with a few more polite pushes, but finally the jerk got under his skin and—much to the delight of the entire auditorium—they tangled and he flattened the guy. In this situation, Mr. B. held his tongue, but the auditorium full of thrilled, supportive students roared.

– SUSAN on Mr. B.

I had a teacher in the fifth grade who had a "puncher gun." Literally a small plastic gun with a fist on it. When you pulled the trigger, the fist extended out. If he caught you not paying attention or doing something you shouldn't be doing, he would sneak up next to you and "punch" you in the head. It didn't hurt, but it certainly got your attention. So not so much "Like my teacher always said . . ." but what my teacher always did, and it worked! He passed away a few years ago, but that will always live on in my memory.

– JENNIFER on Mr. S.

I always tell my students, "Letters make sounds, sounds make words, words make sentences, and sentences tell a story!"

– MADELINE

One night I was watching the news with my dad, like I always did, and a reporter used the word "homosexual." I asked my dad what the word meant and he said, "They're fairies to me" and with that, he changed the station. So the next day during a study hall, I looked up the word "homosexual" in the dictionary. I was confused, so I went up to my fifth-grade teacher, Miss C., and this is how the conversation went.

"Miss C., can you explain this word and its definition to me?" I asked. "Of course," she said, and then looked at the word. She flushed a little, and then told me, "You know how your mom and dad are a married couple?" And of course I said yes. "Well," Miss C. went on, "sometimes this happens between two men or two women."

I said, "WHAT?!" And Miss C. said, "When two people love each other, that is what the word means."

"OK," I said, shocked. And Miss C. continued, "NO more words today, Gary!"

As the years went by, I began to suspect that Miss C. was gay, though of course I hadn't realized it at the time. She used to play basketball with our neighbor, Kay, from across the street. My mom would say, "Miss C. is across the street with Kay again. She should let her hair grow longer."

All this to say that I have Miss C. from the fifth grade to thank for explaining this word—a word that I would later realize describes me—without prejudice before my parents or I were ready to open that door.

– GARY on Miss C.

My music teacher would tell us, "Don't settle for your present level of achievement." And he would also urge us to "make mistakes loudly," so that we could hear them and fix them.

– JON on Mr. T.

I am a kindergarten teacher in a low-income, transient neighborhood where the students are ethnically and educationally very diverse. Some students are reading, while others have never seen a letter or number before. I work really hard to get them on a schedule and routine in order to make them feel comfortable and ready for learning. Once that routine is established (which is exhausting and tedious) we relish the regularity of it. Students know their expectations and what boundaries they can push with me and how I will react. Some days life happens and we veer off course from our delicate schedule. When we have an assembly that might cut down their free time at the end of the day, or there's a planned fire/lockdown drill, I always give them a heads up that it will be a "go with the flow" day. Some of my students have chaotic lives and school is the happiest/most structured time for them. Kids like being in the loop, being spoken to as humans, not just as little kids. The "go with the flow" advice also doesn't focus on the change or diminish it—

it simply says, "Hey, here's a change, not a big deal, but we're going to rock it and still behave like we know we should." My students will rise to the occasion when given the opportunity to do so. And now I find myself telling my friends to "go with the flow," which has an implied message of "It will all be all right."

– ALISON

"Life IS all about the chi."

– ERL, high school advisor, to Martha

When we were nagging her, my fourth-grade teacher, Ms. G., always said, "Vamoose, goose!"

– KASEEM on Ms. G.

At the art academy where I taught, I had three sayings on the blackboard that I always had the students recite:

1. Pray for Wisdom.

2. Surround Yourself with Beauty.

3. Repetition—Confidence—Passion.

I usually explained each with this verbal support:

Pray for Wisdom—everything else will fall into place, including success.

Surround Yourself with Beauty—that means music, the environment, people, thoughts, etc.

Repetition—use this in your studies and practicing, and you will get to the passion that makes life a joy.

Corny? Hokey? Maybe, but the kids sure loved it!

– DR. B.

"Some people just walk to the beat of a different drummer. And you are one of those people. Stay away from math. Music and writing are your strengths. Embrace them." I did. And she was right.

– SISTER R. to Denise

9

THE OLD STANDARDS

There are books of quotations that cover adages and sayings from everywhere under the sun and from throughout history. And then there is the glossary of "teachers' pets," the old saws that every pupil has heard from time immemorial.

"EMPTY BARRELS MAKE A LOT OF NOISE."

– MRS. J. to Jane

Here is what I say to my wonderful students who are learning to read: "I could listen to you read all day. Please read that to me again."

– ELIZABETH

"ENUNCIATE!"

– MRS. T to Nancy

Throughout the years,
I seemed to hear a lot of
that old teacher favorite,
"A word to the wise
is sufficient."

– JANE

I was only in sixth grade and making my mark.
Mrs. McL. said more than once, "Clifford, you are
rude, crude, and insubordinate."

– CLIFF on Mrs. McL.

"There is a poster in my classroom, and I let it speak for me. It says:

IT'S NOT FAIR.
IT'S NOT MY FAULT.
I DIDN'T KNOW.

After those three phrases, do you have anything else to say?"

– SUE

"Patience is a virtue, Miss B.,
and you do not have it!"
She was correct.

– KELLY on Ms. M.

"MS. COHEN—
ELEVATE YOUR MIND
FROM THE GUTTER."

– MR. X to Leslie

"You don't have the brains the good Lord gave a blue jay."

– MRS. T., an avid ornithologist
and fifth-grade teacher, to Scott

"You would lose your head if it weren't screwed on."
(She was my favorite teacher of all time.)

– MISS H. to Cindie

"Andy, do you always have to
be so goddamn cynical?"

– MR. C., a high school English teacher, to Andy

"I know your parents taught
you better than that."

– MRS. L. to Chimere
....

10

OUCH!

Though we agree that teachers are saviors and angels and heroes all rolled into one (and we tip our hat!), somehow they manage to be human, too—and with that come the mistakes and pratfalls that we all encounter.

"You're very smart—you'd be a great secretary to a senator in Washington someday." Not even a legislative aide! Sheesh.

– MR. F. to Sara

Our chorus teacher used to say, "If you died tomorrow, would you be happy with the way that last piece sounded?" No pressure!

– MERLE on Miss P.

Mrs. R., my fourth-grade teacher, once said to me—in front of the whole class—"Louisa J., you are the BOSSIEST child I have ever seen!" It didn't feel so great at the time, but now I remember it with a kind of pride. And I like telling the story to my own students.

– LOUISA on Mrs. R.

"You have such a beautiful smile. You should smile during the spring choral performance instead of moving your mouth and singing."

– SISTER M. to Noreen

MY ACTING TEACHER SAID I SHOULD STICK TO MODELING.

– JAYNE on Mr. B.

I told a teacher that I had yelled at my son for misbehaving, causing him to run off and hide. Nothing too scary, but I was beginning to get a *little* nervous when I finally found him. "Try your medium voice," she advised.

– ANN on Mrs. R.

My high school English teacher repeatedly told me, "You're a pimple on the ass of progress."

– MARTHA on Mr. R.

"If you want someone to say it's beautiful, take it home and show it to your mother."

– MR. S., art teacher, to Eric

I had a high school teacher who was onto me from the start. She'd say, "Learn to control your face, Faith. I can read your thoughts in every expression."

– FAITH on Mrs. S.

Every time I go to an art museum, I still hear him say, "I know you could have done that, but *he* did it!"

– WELLS on Mr. B.

Perhaps it's fair to say I was a stickler in school. At one point, I bugged my teacher about a grade so much that he finally said, "You really have to have the extra point? Go ahead, take it."

– JODY on Mr. L.

My fifth-grade music teacher
told me, in front of the rest of the
class, that my voice was so bad
that I could no longer sing aloud,
I had to mouth the words!

– MEG on Mrs. K.

One teacher said I had a sunny
disposition. One out of twelve.

– SUSAN on one (out of twelve) of her teachers

Sometimes teachers seem to be a little less *with it* than the kids they're teaching, provoking roomfuls of snickers that they just don't understand. This was the problem for my band teacher, who would inevitably say to his assembled musicians, baton aloft, "All right, kids, get ready. I'll beat off."

– DIANE on Mr. H.

Mr. N., my history and philosophy teacher, would often joke that "You have to hand it to the Venus de Milo."

– ROBBIE on Mr. N.

Before we went onstage for our third-grade concert, Mrs. S. announced: "Okay, some of us are singers and some of us are listeners. Amy, you're a listener."

– AMY on Mrs. S.

A teacher once said to us in frustration, "I give you guys three feet, and you take a yard!"

– PAT on Mr. M.

My gym teacher used to have us do chest exercises while chanting, "We must, we must, we must improve our bust!" This was clearly a long time ago.

– SUSAN on Mrs. B.

My number one admonishment to my students is, "'Can't' is not allowed in this room."

– JANA

"Your test scores are amazing. Now, how can I get you to come to class?"

– MR. A. to Aiisha

LIFE CHANGERS

If you're lucky, you've met at least one person on your journey to being an adult who has helped you make the right turns at crucial times. A teacher who taught you that ineffable *something* that may have actually set your life on a different course, or clocked your world just a little. Nevertheless, he or she changed you forever.

I had just moved to Florida from Brooklyn, and Ms. S. took a special interest in me. "You can write," she said, explaining that she wanted to move me into the honors English class. But because of scheduling conflicts, transferring wasn't an option. So instead, she told me to ignore everything she wrote on the blackboard for the rest of the year. "Ignore the discussions. Ignore the assignments. You're going to sit here and do the honors work."

A decade later, when my first novel was published, I went back to her classroom and knocked on the door. "Can I help you?" she asked, trying to place me. I'd had a lot more hair the last time we saw each other. "My name is Brad Meltzer," I said, handing her a copy of my book. "And I wrote this for you."

Ms. S. began to cry. She'd been considering early retirement, she said, because she felt she wasn't having enough of an impact on her students.

I didn't know how to make Ms. S. understand what she'd done for me. Thanks to her, I fell in love with Shakespeare—In fact, she once forced me to read the part of Romeo while a girl I had a crush on read Juliet—and I learned how to compose an essay. It was her belief in me that gave me the confidence to become a writer. I owed her.

Thirteen years later, when I heard that she was finally ready to retire, you better believe I was at her going-away party. It felt a little like sneaking into the faculty lounge: I wanted to surprise her, so I tried to blend in.

I was hiding in a corner when one of the teachers called everyone's attention to the presentation of a parting gift—a crystal vase. All Ms. S. needed to do was say a few words thanking everyone for coming. Instead, she stood up and delivered a stem-winding speech that began like this:

"For those of you complaining that kids have changed, and that it's harder to teach these days, you're getting old. You're getting lazy. These kids haven't changed, you have! Do. Not. Give. Up. On. These. Kids!"

When she finished her rallying cry, the crowd burst into applause, and I was ready to apply for a teaching certificate. That was the woman I remembered! I went up to Ms. S. and thanked her for changing my life all those years ago. I realized that night that I was still, and would forever be, her student.

Oh, and my crush who read the part of Juliet? I married her. I owe Ms. S. for that, too.

— BRAD on Ms. S.

I was a math major, and one of only three students in one of Dr. K.'s advanced math classes. As it was a morning class, and it was college, I cut it perhaps more than I should have. The professor finally suggested that if I was going to be a no-show, I could at least have the courtesy to call the other two students so they could both sleep in, too.

– TOM on Dr. K.

I grew up in the projects in the South Bronx,
a very rough neighborhood. But I was lucky
enough to have a teacher in high school who
always told me, "You have potential." Though
I kept asking him what he meant, he'd never
really answer. But over the years, he opened up
all kinds of opportunities for me. With his help,
I became editor of the school paper and I got a
scholarship to New York University. Finally, in
my senior year, I approached him and said, "I'm
about to graduate, and I'm going to ask you one
more time: What is the potential you keep saying you see in me? Won't you tell me now?" He
replied at last, "It was that you never said no."

– KAREN on Mr. S.

In the early seventies, during a history lesson on Henry VIII, my teacher said, "If Henry had a problem with a wife, he either divorced her or silenced her by cutting off her head. Funny how things haven't progressed that much for women." I felt she had her own bit of personal history she was sharing at the time. She was amazing and fostered my love of history, especially European history. She always made time for me after class when I had questions and is responsible for my fascination with Marie Antoinette.

– WILL on Mrs. R.

I remember my drama teacher with more and more respect as I grow older. He was unusually honest for an adult! After I complained that he didn't critique the boys in the play as harshly as he did the girls, he said, "There will always be more parts for boys than boys who want to play them and too many girls for the few female roles, so you girls have to be better because you have more competition." A life lesson indeed.

– SUSAN on Mr. P.

"It's frivolous."

When Mr. B. was retired, but still teaching English part time, senior skip day still bugged him—NO seniors showed up on that day. Ever. The kids adored him—he expected a lot and he was a tough grader, but he always pushed them to be their best. He was so good that the kids even realized it when they were students—no waiting until they got older and wiser!

Every student knew Mr. B. HATED senior skip day because he worried something would happen to one of them, plus, he always insisted, "It's frivolous." The closest he came to tears during his career was the morning of his last year of teaching when he went to his 8:30 AM Senior English classroom on senior skip day, shoulders drooping . . . and every single seat was filled because it mattered so much to him and the students loved him and wanted to show their respect. After that, they all immediately left for the rest of the day to join their friends. But the tip of the hat was there.

– SUSAN on Mr. B.

When I was in eleventh grade, my English teacher called me into his classroom after school and introduced me to the editor of our high school literary magazine. He said to her, "Here's the boy who wrote that beautiful poem," referring to some piece of sonorous juvenilia I had coughed up and would be mortified to see again now. I was drunk on sounds with more ambition than talent, but nevertheless, who can forget the rush of first praise? The next year, thanks to Mr. P., I found myself in charge of that magazine. He was a wonderful teacher, and I would remember him as such even apart from his being responsible for one of my first moments of literary elation, that thrilling moment when somebody recognizes you for something you wrote and you begin to fashion an identity around what you have created. Parents love their children simply for their existence, but teachers love their students for what they see them discovering and learning to do. I wish there would have been more occasions and better poems for Mr. P. to extol, but more than that, I wish I had known where he was in his retirement so I could thank him.

– CHIP, upon reading Mr. P.'s obituary

ACKNOWLEDGMENTS

In putting together a book like this, naturally my biggest help comes from all the contributors. I reach out through email, word of mouth, social media, and believe it or not, people who I meet throughout my day as a bookseller. For this book, I talked to them about their school years, and what they remembered, good or bad. As you can imagine, it's a rich stew of funny, scary, and inspiring.

Whether in person or electronically, the folks who chimed in—and so often the friends *they* reached out to for stories—are the heart of the book. I thank every one of you for reaching back in your memories and sharing.

But a bunch of stories are just the same as sitting around a campfire, unless you've got a great publishing partner, as I do in Abrams Books. From old friends Michael Jacobs and Mary Wowk to slightly newer comrades-in-arms like Maya Bradford, Melissa Esner, Devin Grosz, John Gall, and all the rest of the team that make every project we do together a labor of love for me. And especially to my editor, David Cashion, who will even occasionally put up with me after hours.

Of course the biggest round of applause goes to teachers of every stripe, everywhere. Where would any of us be without you? There aren't enough thanks in the world for what you do.

ABOUT THE AUTHOR

Erin McHugh is a former publishing executive and the award-winning author of more than twenty books of trivia, history, children's titles, and other subjects, including *One Good Deed: 365 Days of Trying to Be Just a Little Bit Better* and *Like My Father Always Said*. . . . She lives in New York City.